A BRIEF INTRODUCTION TO SOME OF THE MANY CHARACTERS WHO APPEAR IN THE ACTS OF THE APOSTLES

WALLACE JACOB

INDIA • SINGAPORE • MALAYSIA

ISBN
Paperback 979-8-89673-841-1
Hardcase 979-8-89699-980-5

Table of Contents

Preface

A number of people with the name '*Simon*' appear in the Holy Bible. For example,

i. Simon Peter – an apostle to whom Lord Jesus said, "*you are a rock, and on this rock foundation I will build my church,..." (Matthew 16:18),*

ii. Simon the Patriot *(Matthew 10:4),*

iii. Simon – who used to live in Bethany. Jesus was in Bethany in Simon's house where a woman came with an alabaster jar filled with an expensive perfume, which she poured on Jesus' head *(Matthew 26:6-7),*

iv. Simon of Cyrene – the soldiers forced him to carry Jesus' cross *(Matthew 27:32),*

v. Simon Iscariot – Judas Iscariot's father *(John 6:71),*

vi. Simon – a magician who used to live in Samaria *(The Acts of the Apostles 8:9),*

vii. Simon – a tanner of leather who used to live in Joppa (*The Acts of the Apostles 9:43).*

A person by the name of Simon also appears in Matthew, Chapter 13, verse 55.

The apostle Philip appears in Chapter 1, verse 13 of *The Acts of the Apostles*. One more follower of the Lord by the name of Philip (he was one of the seven helpers chosen to handle finances because the apostles wanted to focus on preaching of God's word) appears in Chapter 6, verse 5 of *The*

Acts of the Apostles. Now, Philip is mentioned in Chapter 8 of *The Acts of the Apostles*. Which Philip is being referred to in Chapter 8? Perhaps, it would be advisable to read a few other holy books authored by people who lived during Lord Jesus' time and shortly afterwards in order to gain an understanding of the persons who appear in *The Acts of the Apostles*.

I am not having information of other holy books authored by people who lived during Lord Jesus' time and/or shortly afterwards. There have been several historians (authors), for example, Josephus (author of *Testimonium Flavianum*), Thallus, Julius Africanus, Gaius Suetonius Tranquillus (there could be many others) who have written about the time when Jesus lived. I have not been able to access their books. There are uncials (which I have not read), for example, *Codex Alexandrinus, Codex Bezae, Codex Claromontanus, Codex Laudianus, Codex Ephraemi Syri rescriptus, Codex Sinaiticus, Codex Vaticanus, Codex Washingtonianus, Codex Koridethianus* which provide vital information pertaining to Christianity. Two thieves were crucified along with Lord Jesus. Perhaps one of the thieves was Gestas and the other was Dismas (or Dysmas). Dismas accepted that he was at fault. (The names of the two thieves perhaps appear in *The Gospel of Nicodemus. The Gospel of Nicodemus* is also referred to as *Acts of Pilate*.) I have not read *The Gospel of Nicodemus*. I have referred to Good News Bible published by St Pauls. There could be several holy books and texts in the Vatican City and other holy locations/places. I feel that in order to gain an understanding of any holy book it is imperative to know the people who appear in the text. Therefore, this book is written. I do not claim to have any knowledge of hermeneutics. I do not make any claim pertaining to the authenticity of this book. I do not challenge any authority in any way. I am not trying to prove or disprove anything. I admit that I am a very weak human being with very little or almost no knowledge or understanding.

This book is only a humble attempt on my part to provide a very brief introduction to some of the people who appear in *The Acts of the Apostles*. A number of holy books have to be studied for gaining a deeper understanding of *The Acts of the Apostles*.

Some experts/authorities might object to the statement "A number of holy books have to be studied for gaining a deeper understanding of *The Acts of the Apostles*." I would like to offer a simple analogy. Can we learn everything about chemical engineering or civil engineering or electrical engineering or mechanical engineering or architecture or law or accountancy from a single book? I don't think that the answer might be in the affirmative. Can we learn everything about medicine from a single book? I don't think that the answer might be in the affirmative. In fact, just like other disciplines there are several specializations and super-specializations in the domain of medicine, such as: General Medicine, Forensic Medicine, Obstetrics and Gynaecology, Anesthesiology, Pediatrics, Cardiology, Neurology, Urology, Dermatology,.... Which implies that perhaps we might have to read many holy books in order to understand the origins of Christianity.

Not everything that Lord Jesus did in his lifetime is recorded. *"Now, there are many other things that Jesus did. If they were all written down one by one, I suppose that the whole world could not hold the books that would be written"* (John 21:25).

There have been changes in the world before and after the crucifixion of Lord Jesus. For instance, the province of Judea was renamed Syria Palestinia almost two centuries after Lord Jesus' birth. Thus, it becomes imperative to acquire knowledge from different sources in order to understand the Holy Word of God.

Let us humbly request the Almighty for grace and blessings so that we might be able to comprehend God's word. The Holy Bible is the Word of God.

[Note: Cornelius Tacitus was a noted historian. Tacitus was born circa 55-56 A.D. Tacitus authored *Dialogus de Oratoribus, Agricola, Germania, Histories, Annales*. In Chapter 44 of Book XV, Tacitus has written that Christus suffered a death penalty in the reign of Tiberius by sentence of the procurator Pontius Pilatus (I referred to: https://penelope.uchicago.edu/Thayer/E/Roman/Texts/Tacitus/Annals/15B*.html for information in this note).]

Pax vobiscum, pax et bonum

Wallace Jacob

Acknowledgments

I thank the Almighty for this booklet. I thank all the religious who show the Way.

Wallace Jacob

A Brief Introduction to Some of the Many People Mentioned in *The Acts of the Apostles*

The Acts of the Apostles is a continuation of *The Gospel according to Luke.* For forty days after his death Lord Jesus appeared to the apostles in many ways. After the ascension of Lord Jesus, the Holy Spirit filled the apostles (on the day of the Pentecost). This article provides a brief introduction to some of the numerous people who appear in *The Acts of the Apostles.*

Sr. No.	Name	Brief introduction	Chapter in *The Acts of the Apostles*
1.	Theophilus	The person to whom *The Acts of the Apostles* is addressed.	Chapter 1
2.	John	John the Baptist (who baptized Jesus in the Jordan).	Chapter 1
3.	Two men dressed in white	They explained to the apostles that Jesus who was taken into heaven would come back in the same way.	Chapter 1
4.	Peter	son of John. Peter is also known by the names Simon (*Matthew 4:18*) and Cephas (*John 1:42*). Simon and Andrew were brothers and both were fishermen.	Chapter 1

Sr. No.	Name	Brief introduction	Chapter in *The Acts of the Apostles*
5.	John	son of Zebedee. John and James were brothers and both were fishermen.	Chapter 1
6.	James	son of Zebedee. Herod got James put to death by the sword.	Chapter 1
7.	Andrew	Peter's brother. Andrew and Peter were from Bethsaida.	Chapter 1
8.	Philip	apostle of Jesus. Philip was from Bethsaida. Philip brought Nathanael to Jesus. (Another holy person by the name of Philip appears in *The Acts of the Apostles* 6:5).	Chapter 1
9.	Thomas	apostle of Jesus.	Chapter 1
10.	Bartholomew	apostle of Jesus.	Chapter 1
11.	Matthew	apostle of Jesus.	Chapter 1
12.	James	apostle of Jesus and son of Alphaeus.	Chapter 1
13.	Simon (the Patriot)	apostle of Jesus.	Chapter 1
14.	Judas	apostle of Jesus and son of James.	Chapter 1
15.	Mary	mother of Lord Jesus. (Some women also accompanied Mary).	Chapter 1
16.	believers	approximately hundred and twenty in number.	Chapter 1
17.	David	son of Jesse. David is a figure of the Old Testament.	Chapter 1
18.	Judas	son of Simon Iscariot.	Chapter 1

Sr. No.	Name	Brief introduction	Chapter in *The Acts of the Apostles*
19.	Joseph (also called Barsabbas and Justus)	Joseph and Matthias accompanied the group during the whole time that Lord Jesus travelled about, beginning from the time John preached his message of baptism until the day Jesus ascended into heaven.	Chapter 1
20.	Matthias	Matthias was added to the group of eleven apostles. Matthias, thus replaced Judas Iscariot.	Chapter 1
21.	Joel (Peter spoke to the large crowd about what the prophet Joel had spoken)	prophet. Joel was the son of Pethuel. Joel had described a terrible invasion of locusts and a devastating drought in Palestine.	Chapter 2
22.	Lame beggar	Peter ordered (and helped) the lame beggar walk by the name of Jesus Christ of Nazareth. The 'lame beggar' was over forty years old.	Chapter 2
23.	Abraham	Abraham's initial name was Abram. The Lord changed Abram's name when Abram was ninety-nine years of age. Abram was the son of Terah.	Chapter 3
24.	Isaac	son of Abraham and Sarah.	Chapter 3
25.	Jacob	son of Isaac and Rebecca. Jacob had twelve sons.	Chapter 3

Sr. No.	Name	Brief introduction	Chapter in *The Acts of the Apostles*
26.	Pilate	(Pontius Pilate) Roman governor.	Chapter 3
27.	a murderer	murderer refers to Barabbas	Chapter 3
28.	Moses	son of a man and a woman from the tribe of Levi (*Exodus*).	Chapter 3
29.	Samuel	son of Elkanah and Hannah.	Chapter 3
30.	some priests, the officer in charge of the temple guards and some Sadducees	were annoyed because Peter and John were teaching the people that Jesus had arisen from the dead. So they arrested Peter and John and put them in jail until the next day.	Chapter 4
31.	Annas	High Priest	Chapter 4
32.	Caiaphas	High Priest (*Matthew 26:57*).	Chapter 4
33.	John	It is difficult to gather much information about John from a statement a part of which reads "the Jewish leaders, the elders, and the teachers of the Law met Annas, Caiaphas, John, Alexander and others who belonged to the High Priest's family."	Chapter 4
34.	Alexander	It is difficult to gather much information about Alexander from a statement a part of which reads "the Jewish leaders, the elders, and the teachers of the Law met Annas, Caiaphas, John, Alexander and others who belonged to the High Priest's family."	Chapter 4

Sr. No.	Name	Brief introduction	Chapter in *The Acts of the Apostles*
35.	Herod	ruler of Galilee (*Luke 23:6*).	Chapter 4
36.	Joseph	a Levite born in Cyprus. The apostles addressed him as Barnabas (which means "One who Encourages"). Joseph sold the field he owned and handed over the money to the apostles.	Chapter 4
37.	Ananias	Sapphira's husband. Ananias and Sapphira sold some property that belonged to them. With his wife's agreement Ananias kept part of the money for himself and handed the rest over to the apostles. Ananias was reproached by Peter and Ananias fell down dead.	Chapter 5
38.	Sapphira	Ananias' wife. Approximately three hours after the death of Ananias, Sapphira came to Peter. When Peter asked her, "Tell me, was this the full amount you and your husband received for your property?", she answered, "Yes, the full amount." She was reproached by Peter for the lie she had spoken after which she fell down at Peter's feet and died.	Chapter 5

Sr. No.	Name	Brief introduction	Chapter in *The Acts of the Apostles*
39.	Gamaliel (Paul was a student of Gamaliel. Paul had received strict instruction in Law) Gamaliel spoke to the Council about Theudas and Judas.	a Pharisee. Gamaliel was a teacher of the Law. When the members of the Council wanted to have the apostles put to death, it was Gamaliel who gave the examples of Theudas and Judas and prevented the council members from having the apostles put to death.	Chapter 5
40.	Theudas	Theudas claimed to be someone great. About four hundred men joined him. Theudas was killed and his followers were scattered and his movement died out.	Chapter 5
41.	Judas	a Galilean. Judas appeared during the time of the census. He drew a crowd after him, but he was killed and all his followers were scattered.	Chapter 5

Sr. No.	Name	Brief introduction	Chapter in *The Acts of the Apostles*
42.	Stephen (Stephen performed great miracles and wonders among the people. Stephen was opposed by some men who were members of the synagogue of the Freedmen. Stephen was stoned to death and Saul approved of his murder.)	one of the seven men who were chosen to handle finances so that the apostles could focus on preaching God's word. There was a quarrel between the Greek-speaking Jews and the native Jews. The Greek speaking Jews claimed that the widows in their sect were being neglected in the daily distribution of funds. Therefore, the apostles suggested that seven men who are known to be full of the Holy Spirit be chosen to handle the finances.	Chapter 6 The stoning of Stephen to death is described in Chapter 7
43.	Philip (the evangelist) Philip is mentioned in Chapter 21 also.	one of the seven men who were chosen to handle finances so that the apostles could devote their full time to prayer and preaching of God's word. Philip had four unmarried daughters who proclaimed God's message.	Chapter 6

Sr. No.	Name	Brief introduction	Chapter in *The Acts of the Apostles*
44.	Prochorus	one of the seven men who were chosen to handle finances so that the apostles could devote their full time to prayer and preaching of God's word.	Chapter 6
45.	Nicanor	one of the seven men who were chosen to handle finances so that the apostles could devote their full time to prayer and preaching of God's word.	Chapter 6
46.	Timon	one of the seven men who were chosen to handle finances so that the apostles could devote their full time to prayer and preaching of God's word.	Chapter 6
47.	Parmenas	one of the seven men who were chosen to handle finances so that the apostles could devote their full time to prayer and preaching of God's word.	Chapter 6
48.	Nicolaus	a Gentile from Antioch who had earlier been converted to Judaism. Nicolaus was also one of the seven men who were chosen to handle finances so that the apostles could devote their full time to prayer and preaching of God's word.	Chapter 6

Sr. No.	Name	Brief introduction	Chapter in *The Acts of the Apostles*
49.	Joseph	one of Jacob's sons. Joseph's brothers threw him into a dry well. Later Joseph's brothers pulled him out of the well and sold him for twenty pieces of silver to the Ishmaelites who took him to Egypt.	Chapter 7
50.	Hamor (Jacob bought a part of a field from the descendants of Hamor for a hundred pieces of silver)	father of Shechem. Hamor and Shechem were killed by Simeon and Levi (brothers of Dinah).	Chapter 7
51.	King of Egypt	had issued a command to all his people: "Take every new-born Hebrew boy and throw him into the Nile, but let all the girls live."	Chapter 7
52.	King of Egypt's daughter	She adopted a baby and gave him the name Moses.	Chapter 7
53.	Aaron (Aaron and Moses were brothers. Aaron was three years elder to Moses)	son of Amram and Jochebed. Amram was the son of Kohath. (Kohath had four sons.) Kohath was the son of Levi.	Chapter 7

Sr. No.	Name	Brief introduction	Chapter in *The Acts of the Apostles*
54.	Joshua (According to *Sirach Chapter 49, verse 12,* Joshua was the son of Jehozadak)	Joshua was the son of Nun. Joshua was Moses' helper. Later Joshua became Moses' successor.	Chapter 7
55.	Solomon	second son of David and Bathsheba.	Chapter 7
56.	Saul (also known as Paul, *The Acts of the Apostles, Chapter 13, verse 9)*	Initially Saul tried to destroy the church; going from house to house, he dragged out the believers, both men and women, and threw them into jail. Saul was a Jew, born in Tarsus in Cilicia. Paul was a Roman citizen.	Chapter 8 Paul was a Jew, born in Tarsus in Cilicia (Chapter 21, Chapter 22).
57.	Simon	a magician. After being baptized Simon stayed close to Philip. Simon offered money to Peter and John asking for power so that anyone he placed his hands on would receive the Holy Spirit. Peter reproached Simon and asked him to repent.	Chapter 8

Sr. No.	Name	Brief introduction	Chapter in *The Acts of the Apostles*
58.	Ethiopian Official	The Ethiopian eunuch was an important official in charge of the treasury of the queen of Ethiopia. He was baptized by Philip.	Chapter 8
59.	Ananias	was a Christian in Damascus. The Lord commanded Ananias to go to the house of Judas (on Straight Street) and place his hands on Saul so that Saul might see again	Chapter 9
60.	Judas	Saul stayed in Judas' house for some time.	Chapter 9
61.	Barnabas (Barnabas went to Antioch, Tarsus)	Saul went to Jerusalem and tried to join the disciples. But the disciples were afraid of him. Then Barnabas helped Saul and took him to the apostles.	Chapter 9
62.	Aeneas	Aeneas was paralysed and had not been able to get out of bed for eight years. Peter said to Aeneas, "Jesus Christ makes you well. Get up and make your bed." At once Aeneas got up.	Chapter 9
63.	Tabitha (Tabitha's name in Greek is Dorcas)	used to live in Joppa. She became ill and died. Peter knelt down and prayed. He turned to Tabitha's body and said, "Tabitha, get up!". Tabitha opened her eyes.	Chapter 9

Sr. No.	Name	Brief introduction	Chapter in *The Acts of the Apostles*
64.	Simon	a tanner of leather. Peter stayed in Simon's house in Joppa for many days. Simon's house was by the sea.	Chapter 9
65.	Cornelius	used to live in Caesarea. Cornelius was a captain in the Roman regiment called "The Italian Regiment." Cornelius sent two of his house servants and a soldier to Peter (in Joppa). Cornelius was given instructions by an angel.	Chapter 10
66.	John	John the Baptist was the son of Zechariah and Elizabeth.	Chapter 11
67.	Agabus	by the power of the Sprit, Agabus predicted that a severe famine was about to come over all the earth. His prediction came true when Claudius was the emperor.	Chapter 11
68.	Herod	Herod Agrippa I was the ruler of Palestine. He had James, the brother of John, put to death by the sword. He arrested Peter and Peter was put into jail. Later an angel of the Lord struck Herod down, because Herod did not give honour to God. Herod was eaten by worms and died.	Chapter 12

Sr. No.	Name	Brief introduction	Chapter in *The Acts of the Apostles*
69.	an angel of the Lord	the angel woke Peter up and led Peter out of the prison and then left Peter.	Chapter 12
70.	Mary	the mother of John Mark.	Chapter 12
71.	Rhoda	a servant-girl.	Chapter 12
72.	Blastus	the man in charge of Herod's palace.	Chapter 12
73.	Simeon	called the Black.	Chapter 13
74.	Lucius	was from Cyrene.	Chapter 13
75.	Manaen	he had been brought up with Herod.	Chapter 13
76.	John Mark	initially helped Barnabas and Saul.	Chapter 13
77.	Bar-Jesus (in Greek his name is Elymas)	was a magician. He was a Jew who claimed to be a prophet. Elymas tried to turn the governor of Paphos away from the faith. Paul cursed Elymas *"you will be blind and will not see the light of day for a time."* At once Elymas felt a dark mist cover his eyes.	Chapter 13
78.	Sergius Paulus	governor of Paphos (an island).	Chapter 13
79.	Saul	son of Kish from the tribe of Benjamin.	Chapter 13

Sr. No.	Name	Brief introduction	Chapter in *The Acts of the Apostles*
80.	a man who had been lame from birth	This man listened to Paul's words in a place by the name of Lystra. Paul said to him, "Stand up straight on your feet!" The man jumped up and started walking around.	Chapter 14
81.	Zeus	Barnabas was given the name Zeus by the crowd in Lystra.	Chapter 14
82.	Hermes	Paul was given the name Hermes by the crowd in Lystra	Chapter 14
83.	Judas (called Barsabbas)	a prophet. Judas accompanied Paul and Barnabas.	Chapter 15
84.	Silas	a prophet. Silas accompanied Paul and Barnabas. Barnabas took Mark and sailed off for Cyprus. Paul chose Silas. Paul went through Syria and Cilicia.	Chapter 15
85.	Timothy (Timothy is mentioned in Chapter 20 also)	a Christian. Timothy's mother, who was also a Christian, was Jewish. Timothy's father was a Greek. All the believers in Lystra and Iconium spoke well of Timothy.	Chapter 16
86.	Lydia	was from Thyatira. Lydia was a dealer in purple cloth. Lydia was a woman who worshipped God. She invited Paul and his companions (Silas, Timothy and Luke) saying, "Come and stay in my house if you have decided that I am a true believer in the Lord."	Chapter 16

Sr. No.	Name	Brief introduction	Chapter in *The Acts of the Apostles*
87.	slave-girl	the slave-girl was possessed by an evil spirit that enabled her to predict the future. She earned a lot of money for her owners by telling fortunes. She followed Paul and his companions shouting, "These men are servants of the Most High God! They announce to you how you can be saved! She did this for many days, until Paul became so upset that he turned round and said to the spirit, "In the name of Jesus Christ I order you to come out of her!" The spirit went out of her that very moment.	Chapter 16
88.	owners of the slave-girl	When the owners of the slave-girl realized that their chance of making money was gone, they seized Paul and Silas and dragged them to the authorities in the public square. The brought them before the Roman officials and said, "These men are Jews, and they are causing trouble in our city. They are teaching customs that are against our law; we are Roman citizens, and we cannot accept these customs or practice them."	Chapter 16

Sr. No.	Name	Brief introduction	Chapter in *The Acts of the Apostles*
89.	crowd	The owners of the slave-girl incited the crowd and the crowd joined in the attack against Paul and Silas.	Chapter 16
90.	officials	The officials tore the clothes off Paul and Silas and ordered them to be whipped.	Chapter 16
91.	jailer	The jailer was ordered to lock Paul and Silas up tight. The jailer threw Paul and Silas into the inner cell and fastened their feet between heavy blocks of wood. About midnight Paul and Silas were praying and singing hymns to God. All of a sudden there was a violent earthquake, which shook the prison to its foundations. All the doors were opened and the chains fell off all the prisoners. The jailer woke up, and thinking that the prisoners had escaped was about to kill himself with his own sword. But Paul shouted at the top of his voice, "Don't harm yourself! We are all here!" The jailer called for a light, rushed in, and fell trembling at the feet of Paul and Silas. Then he led them out and asked, "Sirs, what must I do to be saved?"	Chapter 16

Sr. No.	Name	Brief introduction	Chapter in *The Acts of the Apostles*
92.	police officers	The Roman authorities sent police officers with the order to release Paul and Silas.	Chapter 16
93.	Jason	Some Jews were jealous of Paul and Silas, and therefore incited some of the loiterers on the streets. They set the whole city in an uproar and attacked Jason's home in their attempt of finding Paul and Silas. But when they did not find Paul and Silas, they dragged Jason and a few other believers before the authorities of the city and made false accusations. They shouted, "These men have caused trouble everywhere! Now they have come to our city, and Jason has kept them in his house. They are all breaking the laws of the Emperor, claiming that there is another king, whose name is Jesus." The authorities made Jason and the others pay a stipulated sum in order to be released.	Chapter 17

Sr. No.	Name	Brief introduction	Chapter in *The Acts of the Apostles*
94.	Certain Epicurean and Stoic teachers	Paul was waiting in Athens for Silas and Timothy. Paul was greatly disturbed when he saw a large number of idols in the city. He, therefore, held deliberations in the synagogue with the Jews and with the Gentiles who worshipped God. Certain Epicurean and Stoic teachers debated with Paul.	Chapter 17
95.	Dionysius	a member of the council. Dionysius joined Paul and believed.	Chapter 17
96.	Damaris	a lady in Athens who believed in Paul's teachings.	Chapter 17
97.	Aquila	was a Jew born in Pontus. He was married to Priscilla. He earned his living by making tents. Paul stayed and worked with them for some time. Aquila and Priscilla left Italy because the Emperor Claudius ordered all the Jews to leave Rome.	Chapter 18
98.	Priscilla	Aquila's wife.	Chapter 18
99.	Claudius	was an emperor. Claudius ordered all the Jews to leave Rome.	Chapter 18
100.	Titius Justus	was a Gentile. Paul lived with Titius for some time.	Chapter 18

Sr. No.	Name	Brief introduction	Chapter in *The Acts of the Apostles*
101.	Crispus	was the leader of a synagogue in Corinth. Crispus, together with all his family; and several other people in Corinth heard the message, believed and were baptized.	Chapter 18
102.	Gallio	Roman governor of Achaia. Gallio refused to be the judge when some Jews seized Paul and took him (Paul) to court saying "*This man is trying to persuade people to worship God in a way that is against the law!*"	Chapter 18
103.	Sosthenes	was a leader of a synagogue. Some Jews seized Sosthenes and beat him in front of the court. When some Jews brought some accusations against Paul, Gallio said, "*If this were a matter of some evil crime or wrong that has been committed, it would be reasonable for me to be patient with you Jews. But since it is an argument about words and names and your own law, you yourselves must settle it. I will not be the judge of such things!*" Gallio drove the Jews out of the court. It was then that the Jews seized Sosthenes and beat him.	Chapter 18

Sr. No.	Name	Brief introduction	Chapter in *The Acts of the Apostles*
104.	Apollos	a Jew who was born in Alexandria. He was an eloquent speaker and had a thorough knowledge of the Scriptures. With his strong arguments he defeated the Jews in public debates by proving from the Scriptures that Jesus is the Messiah.	Chapter 18
105.	approximately twelve disciples	When Paul reached Ephesus he found some disciples. Paul asked them "*Did you receive the Holy Spirit when you became believers?*" The disciples explained that they had not even heard of the existence of a Holy Spirit. When Paul further asked them "*Well, then what kind of baptism did you receive?*", they answered, "*The baptism of John.*" Paul then explained, "*The baptism of John was for those who turned from their sins; and he told the people of Israel to believe in the one who was coming after him–that is, in Jesus.*" When they heard this, they were baptized in the name of Lord Jesus. Paul placed his hands on them, and the Holy Spirit came upon them. They spoke in strange tongues and also proclaimed God's message.	Chapter 19

Sr. No.	Name	Brief introduction	Chapter in *The Acts of the Apostles*
106.	Tyrannus	Paul held discussions in the lecture hall of Tyrannus.	Chapter 19
107.	Sceva	a Jewish Priest.	Chapter 19
108.	Seven brothers	the sons of Sceva. The seven brothers used the name of Lord Jesus for driving out evil spirits. Once when they were trying to drive out an evil spirit from a man, the evil spirit said to the seven brothers, "I know Jesus, and I know about Paul; but you–who are you?" The man who was possessed by the evil spirit attacked the seven brothers and overpowered them all. The seven brothers ran away from the man's house, wounded and with their clothes torn off.	Chapter 19
109.	some people who had practised magic (and lived in Ephesus)	brought their books together and burnt them in public. They added up the price of the books, and the total came to fifty thousand silver coins.	Chapter 19
110.	Erastus (Erastus is mentioned in *Paul's Letter to the Romans 16:23*)	Paul's helper. Paul sent him to Macedonia.	Chapter 19

Sr. No.	Name	Brief introduction	Chapter in *The Acts of the Apostles*
111.	Demetrius	a silversmith. Demetrius made silver models of the temple of the goddess Artemis and his business meant profits to his workers. He, therefore called his workers and other workers who performed similar work and incited them by saying "*Men, you know that our prosperity comes from this work. Now, you can see and hear for yourselves what this fellow Paul is doing. He says that man-made gods are not gods at all, and he has succeeded in convincing many people, both here in Ephesus and in nearly the whole province of Asia. There is the danger, then, that this business of ours will get a bad name. Not only that, but there is also the danger that the temple of the great goddess Artemis will come to mean nothing and that her greatness will be destroyed–the goddess worshipped by everyone in Asia and in all the world!*"	Chapter 19

Sr. No.	Name	Brief introduction	Chapter in *The Acts of the Apostles*
112.	Gaius (Gaius is mentioned in Chapter 20 of *The Acts of the Apostles* also)	When the crowd (workers who used to make models of the temple and the goddess Artemis) heard Demetrius they became furious and started shouting, "*Great is Artemis of Ephesus!*" The ruckus spread throughout the whole city. The mob seized Gaius and Aristarchus, two Macedonians who were travelling with Paul, and rushed them to the theatre. The believers did not allow Paul to go before the crowd.	Chapter 19
113.	Aristarchus (Aristarchus is mentioned in Chapter 20 of *The Acts of the Apostles* also)	When the crowd (people who were incited by Demetrius) heard Demetrius they became furious and started hollering "*Great is Artemis of Ephesus!*" The horde seized Gaius and Aristarchus (two Macedonians who were accompanying Paul) and hurried them to the theatre.	Chapter 19

Sr. No.	Name	Brief introduction	Chapter in *The Acts of the Apostles*
114.	Alexander	a Jew. The crowd (mentioned in 107 and 108) was shouting. Most of them did not even know why they had assembled. Some people concluded that Alexander was responsible since the Jews made him go up to the front. Alexander motioned with his hands for the people to be silent, and he did try to make a speech of defence. But when the crowd understood that Alexander was a Jew, the crowd kept shouting for two hours "*Great is Artemis of Ephesus!*"	Chapter 19

Sr. No.	Name	Brief introduction	Chapter in *The Acts of the Apostles*
115.	town clerk	Eventually the town clerk was successful in pacifying the crowd (mentioned in 107 and 108). The town clerk said *"Fellow-Ephesians! Everyone knows that the city of Ephesus is the keeper of the temple of the great Artemis and of the sacred stone that fell down from heaven. Nobody can deny these things. So then, you must calm down and not do anything reckless. You have brought these men here even though they have not robbed temples or said evil things about our goddess. If Demetrius and his workers have an accusation against anyone, we have the authorities and the regular days for court; charges can be made there. But if there is something more that you want, it will have to be settled in a legal meeting of citizens. For after what has happened today, there is the danger that we will be accused of a riot. There is no excuse for all this uproar, and we would not be able to give a good reason for it."* The town clerk then dismissed the meeting.	Chapter 19

Sr. No.	Name	Brief introduction	Chapter in *The Acts of the Apostles*
116.	Sopater	son of Pyrrhus from Berea.	Chapter 20
117.	Secundus	Secundus waited for Paul and his companions in Troas. Paul and his companions spent a week in Troas.	Chapter 20
118.	Tychicus	Tychicus waited for Paul and his companions in Troas.	Chapter 20
119.	Trophimus	Trophimus waited for Paul and his companions in Troas. Trophimus was from Ephesus.	Chapter 20
120.	Eutychus	One evening (Saturday) when Paul and his companions had gathered together for a fellowship meal, Paul spoke to the people and continued till midnight. Eutychus (a young man) was sitting in the window. Eutychus was overcome with sleep and fell from the third storey to the ground and died. Paul went down, threw himself on Eutychus and hugged him and said "*Don't worry, he is still alive!*" Eutychus was taken home alive.	Chapter 20

Sr. No.	Name	Brief introduction	Chapter in *The Acts of the Apostles*
121.	Agabus	Agabus was a prophet. Agabus arrived in Caesarea from Judaea, took Paul's belt, tied up his own feet and hands with it, and said, "*This is what the Holy Spirit says: The owner of this belt will be tied up in this way by the Jews in Jerusalem, and they will hand him over to the Gentiles.*"	Chapter 21
122.	Mnason	Mnason was from Cyprus. Mnason had been a believer since the early days. Some of the disciples from Caesarea took Paul and his companions to Mnason's house.	Chapter 21
123.	James	When Paul and his companions* reached Jerusalem they were accorded a warm welcome by the believers. The next day Paul and his companions went to see James. *Who are Paul's companions? Sopater son of Pyrrhus, Aristarchus, Secundus, Gaius, Tychicus, Trophimus, and Timothy (Chapter 20, verses 4 to 6).	Chapter 21

Sr. No.	Name	Brief introduction	Chapter in *The Acts of the Apostles*
124.	Four men	The four men had bound themselves with an oath. Paul was supposed to proceed along with them and join them in the ceremony of purification and pay their expenses, after which the four men would be able to shave their heads. In this way everyone would know that Paul himself abided by the law of Moses. Thousands of Jews had become believers and they were very much devoted to the Law. They had been told that Paul had been teaching all the Jews who lived in Gentile countries to abandon the law of Moses, not to circumcise their children and follow the Jewish customs.	Chapter 21

Sr. No.	Name	Brief introduction	Chapter in *The Acts of the Apostles*
125.	some Jews from the province of Asia	When the seven days (which would mark the end of the period of purification for the four men) were about to come to end some Jews from the province of Asia saw Paul in the Temple. They seized Paul and stirred up the whole crowd "Men of Israel! Help! This is the man who goes everywhere teaching everyone against the people of Israel, the Law of Moses, and this Temple. And now he has even brought some Gentiles into the Temple and defiled this holy place!" They said this because they were under the impression that Paul had taken Trophimus into the Temple.	Chapter 21
126.	mob	The mob seized Paul and dragged him out of the Temple. The doors of the Temple were closed and the mob was trying to kill Paul.	Chapter 21

Sr. No.	Name	Brief introduction	Chapter in *The Acts of the Apostles*
127.	commander of the Roman troops	When the mob was trying to kill Paul, a report was sent to the commander of the Roman troops that all Jerusalem was rioting. The commander had become a Roman citizen by paying a large amount of money.	Chapter 21
128.	some officers and soldiers	The commander took some officers and soldiers and rushed down to the crowd. The people stopped beating Paul when they saw the commander with the soldiers. The commander went over to Paul, arrested Paul and ordered that Paul be bound with two chains.	Chapter 21
129.	Egyptian fellow	According to the commander an Egyptian fellow had started an insurrection (a revolution) and led four thousand armed terrorists out into the desert.	Chapter 21
130.	chief priests and the whole Council	The commander wanted to ascertain what the Jews were accusing Paul of, so the next day he ordered that the chains with which Paul was bound be removed and the chief priests and the whole council to meet.	Chapter 22

Sr. No.	Name	Brief introduction	Chapter in *The Acts of the Apostles*
131.	Ananias	was a High Priest. When Paul was made to stand before the chief priests and the Council, he (Paul) said, "My fellow-Israelites! My conscience is perfectly clear about the way in which I have lived before God to this very day." On hearing Paul's statement, Ananias ordered those who were standing close to Paul to strike him on the mouth. Paul remarked, "God will certainly strike you—you whitewashed wall! You sit there to judge me according to the Law, yet you break the Law by ordering them to strike me!"	Chapter 23
132.	the Sadducees and the Pharisees (the Pharisees believe that people will rise from death. The Pharisees also believe in the existence of angels and spirits.)	Paul understood that some people in the group were Sadducees and some people were Pharisees. He therefore said, "Fellow-Israelites! I am a Pharisee, the son of Pharisees. I am on trial here because of the hope I have that the dead will rise to life!" On hearing Paul's statement, the Pharisees and the Sadducees began to quarrel. The Sadducees are of the conviction that people will not rise from death and that there are no angels or spirits.	Chapter 23

Sr. No.	Name	Brief introduction	Chapter in *The Acts of the Apostles*
133.	some Jews (more than forty)	took a vow that they would not eat or drink anything until they had killed Paul. They approached the chief priests and the elders and declared, "We have taken a solemn vow together not to eat a thing until we have killed Paul. Now then, you and the Council send word to the Roman commander to bring Paul down to you, pretending that you want to get more accurate information about him. But we will be ready to kill him before he ever gets here."	Chapter 23
134.	son of Paul's sister	learnt about the plot of the killing of Paul. He went to the fort and made it known to Paul. Paul then spoke to one of the officers, "Take this young man to the commander; he has something to tell him." Paul's sister's son reported the plan to the commander. The name of the commander was Claudius Lysias.	Chapter 23

Sr. No.	Name	Brief introduction	Chapter in *The Acts of the Apostles*
135.	two officers, two hundred soldiers, seventy horsemen, two hundred spearmen. (The foot-soldiers accompanied Paul to Antipatris. The horsemen went with Paul up to Caesarea.)	The commander sent Paul to Felix. Two hundred soldiers, seventy horsemen, two hundred spearmen accompanied Paul for his protection. They left by 09:00 pm. The commander wrote a letter to governor Felix, "Claudius Lysias to His Excellency, the governor Felix: Greetings. The Jews seized this man and were about to kill him. I learnt that he was a Roman citizen, so I went with my soldiers and rescued him. I wanted to know what they were accusing him of, so I took him down to their Council. I found out that he had not done anything for which he deserved to die or be put in prison; the accusation against him had to do with questions about their own law. And when I was informed that there was a plot against him, at once I decided to send him to you. I have told his accusers to make their charges against him before you."	Chapter 23

Sr. No.	Name	Brief introduction	Chapter in *The Acts of the Apostles*
136.	Felix	governor.	Chapter 23
137.	Tertullus	lawyer. Tertullus made his accusations against Paul as follows: "Your Excellency! Your wise leadership has brought us a long period of peace, and many necessary reforms are being made for the good of our country. We welcome this everywhere and at all times, and we are deeply grateful to you. I do not want to take up too much of your time, however, so I beg you to be kind and listen to our brief account. We found this man to be a dangerous nuisance; he starts riots among the Jews all over the world and is a leader of the party of the Nazarenes. He also tried to defile the Temple, and we arrested him. If you question this man, you yourself will be able to learn from him all the things that we are accusing him of." Some Jews also joined in the accusation against Paul.	Chapter 24

Sr. No.	Name	Brief introduction	Chapter in *The Acts of the Apostles*
138.	Lysias	commander. After hearing Paul's version, Felix said, "When the commander Lysias arrives, I will decide your case."	Chapter 24
139.	officer in charge of Paul	Felix ordered the officer in charge of Paul to keep a guard over him (Paul) but allow him some freedom and allow Paul's friends to provide for his (Paul's) needs.	Chapter 24
140.	Drusilla	Felix's wife. Drusilla was a Jew.	Chapter 24
141.	Porcius Festus	succeeded Felix as governor. Felix did not release Paul from prison.	Chapter 24
142.	Chief priests and the Jewish leaders	begged Festus that Paul be allowed to travel to Jerusalem. The chief priests and the Jewish leaders had hatched a plan to kill Paul on the way. (Paul was kept as a prisoner in Caesarea.)	Chapter 25
143.	King Agrippa Agrippa appears in Chapter 26 also.	Agrippa II was the son of Herod Agrippa I. Festus brought Paul's case before Agrippa. Paul tried to defend himself in front of Agrippa.	Chapter 25

Sr. No.	Name	Brief introduction	Chapter in *The Acts of the Apostles*
144.	Bernice Bernice appears in Chapter 26 also.	Bernice was the daughter of Herod Agrippa I.	Chapter 25
145.	Julius	an officer in the Roman army regiment called "The Emperor's Regiment."	Chapter 27
146.	Aristarchus	a Macedonian from Thessalonica.	Chapter 27
147.	an angel of the God	said to Paul, "Don't be afraid, Paul! You must stand before the Emperor. And God in his goodness to you has spared the lives of all those who are sailing with you."	Chapter 27
148.	276 people on board the ship	The ship was from Alexandria and was supposed to sail to Italy.	Chapter 27
149.	natives of Malta	lit a fire and received Paul and his companions.	Chapter 28
150.	Publius	the chief of the island (Malta).	Chapter 28
151.	Publius' father	was in bed. He was suffering from fever and dysentery. Paul went into his room, prayed, placed his hands on him, and healed him.	Chapter 28
152.	sick people on the island	were healed by Paul.	Chapter 28

Sr. No.	Name	Brief introduction	Chapter in *The Acts of the Apostles*
153.	some believers	in the town of Puteoli. Paul and his companions stayed in Puteoli for a week.	Chapter 28
154.	believers in Rome	travelled as far as the towns of Market of Appius and Three Inns to meet Paul and his companions.	Chapter 28
155.	a soldier	In Rome, Paul was allowed to live by himself with a soldier guarding him.	Chapter 28
156.	local Jewish leaders	Paul called the local Jewish leaders to a meeting.	Chapter 28

For two years, Paul lived in a place he rented for himself. He preached about the Kingdom of God and taught about Lord Jesus Christ.

Question: Who/What is Molech? Who/What is Rephan?

Answer: Molech and Rephan (star god) are the idols which the people of Israel had made in order to worship.

Places Mentioned in The Acts of the Apostles

Heaven (Lord Jesus was taken up to heaven)	Chapter 1
Jerusalem	Chapter 1, Chapter 8, Chapter 9, Chapter 11, Chapter 12, Chapter 13, Chapter 16, Chapter 18, Chapter 19, Chapter 20, Chapter 21, Chapter 22, Chapter 24, Chapter 25, Chapter 26, Chapter 28
Judea	Chapter 1, Chapter 2, Chapter 8, Chapter 9, Chapter 11, Chapter 12, Chapter 15, Chapter 21, Chapter 28
Samaria	Chapter 1, Chapter 8, Chapter 9, Chapter 15
Mount of Olives (about half a mile from Jerusalem)	Chapter 1
Akeldama ("Field of Blood") Judas had bought the field	Chapter 1
Parthia	Chapter 2
Media	Chapter 2
Elam	Chapter 2
Mesopotamia	Chapter 2, Chapter 7
Cappadocia	Chapter 2

Pontus	Chapter 2, Chapter 18
Asia	Chapter 2, Chapter 16, Chapter 19, Chapter 20, Chapter 24
Phrygia	Chapter 2, Chapter 16, Chapter 18
Pamphylia	Chapter 2, Chapter 13, Chapter 14, Chapter 15, Chapter 27
Egypt	Chapter 2
regions of Libya near Cyrene	Chapter 2
Rome	Chapter 2, Chapter 18, Chapter 23, Chapter 28
Crete	Chapter 2, Chapter 27
Arabia	Chapter 2
Nazareth	Chapter 2, Chapter 22, Chapter 26
Beautiful Gate { a lame man (later healed by Peter) used to beg the people for money at the Beautiful Gate of the Holy Temple }	Chapter 3
Solomon's Porch	Chapter 3
Haran	Chapter 7
Egypt	Chapter 7, Chapter 13
Canaan	Chapter 7, Chapter13
Shechem	Chapter 7
Midian	Chapter 7
Mount Sinai	Chapter 7
Gaza	Chapter 8
Ethiopia	Chapter 8
Azotus	Chapter 8

Caesarea	Chapter 8, Chapter 9, Chapter 10, Chapter 11, Chapter 12, Chapter 18, Chapter 21, Chapter 23, Chapter 24, Chapter 25
Damascus	Chapter 9, Chapter 22, Chapter 26
Straight Street (in Damascus)	Chapter 9
Tarsus	Chapter 9, Chapter 11, Chapter 21
Galilee	Chapter 9, Chapter 13
Lydda	Chapter 9
Sharon	Chapter 9
Joppa	Chapter 9, Chapter 10, Chapter 11
Phoenicia	Chapter 11, Chapter 15, Chapter 21
Cyprus	Chapter 11, Chapter 13, Chapter 15, Chapter 21, Chapter 27
Antioch	Chapter 11, Chapter 13, Chapter 14, Chapter 15, Chapter 18
Cyrene	Chapter 11, Chapter 13
Tyre	Chapter 12, Chapter 21
Sidon	Chapter 12
Seleucia	Chapter 13
Salamis	Chapter 13
Paphos	Chapter 13
Perga (a city in Pamphylia)	Chapter 13
Pisidia	Chapter 13, Chapter 14
Iconium	Chapter 13, Chapter 14, Chapter 16
Lystra (city in Lycaonia)	Chapter 14, Chapter 16

Derbe (city in Lycaonia)	Chapter 14, Chapter 16, Chapter 20
Perga	Chapter 14
Attalia	Chapter14
Syria	Chapter 15, Chapter 18, Chapter 20, Chapter 21
Cilicia	Chapter 15, Chapter 21, Chapter 22, Chapter 23, Chapter 27
Galatia	Chapter 16, Chapter 18
Mysia	Chapter 16
Bithynia	Chapter 16
Troas	Chapter 16, Chapter 20
Macedonia	Chapter 16, Chapter 18, Chapter 19, Chapter 20
Samothrace	Chapter 16
Neapolis	Chapter 16
Philippi	Chapter 16, Chapter 20
Thyatira	Chapter 16
Amphipolis	Chapter 17
Apollonia	Chapter 17
Thessalonica	Chapter 17, Chapter 20, Chapter 27
Berea	Chapter 17, Chapter 20
Athens	Chapter 17
Areopagus	Chapter 17
Corinth	Chapter 18, Chapter 19
Italy	Chapter 18, Chapter 27
Achaia	Chapter 18, Chapter 19, Chapter 20
Cenchreae	Chapter 18
Ephesus	Chapter 18, Chapter 19, Chapter 20, Chapter 21

Alexandria	Chapter 18, Chapter 27, Chapter 28
Trophimus	Chapter 20
Assos	Chapter 20
Mitylene	Chapter 20
Chios	Chapter 20
Samos	Chapter 20
Miletus	Chapter 20
Cos	Chapter 21
Rhodes	Chapter 21
Patara	Chapter 21
Ptolemais	Chapter 21
Antipatris	Chapter 23
Adramyttium	Chapter 27
Sidon	Chapter 27
Myra (in Lycia)	Chapter 27
Cnidus	Chapter 27
Cape Salmone	Chapter 27
Safe Harbors	Chapter 27
Lasea	Chapter 27
Phoenix (a harbor in Crete that faces southwest and northwest)	Chapter 27
Cauda (island)	Chapter 27
Libya	Chapter 27
Mediterranean	Chapter 27
Malta	Chapter 28
Syracuse	Chapter 28
Rhegium	Chapter 28
Puteoli	Chapter 28
Market of Appius	Chapter 28
Three Inns	Chapter 28

Who were the first Christians?

It was at Antioch that the believers were first called Christians (Acts 11: 26)

What is Areopagus?

Areopagus (The Acts of the Apostles, Chapter 17, verse 19): the city council in Athens.

Paul has written:

Paul's letter to the Romans (the letter begins with: *From Paul, a servant of Christ Jesus . . .*),

Paul's First letter to the Corinthians (the letter begins with: *From Paul, who was called . . .*),

Paul's Second Letter to the Corinthians (the letter begins with: *From Paul, an apostle of Christ Jesus . . .*),

Paul's letter to the Galatians (the letter begins with: *From Paul, whose call to be an apostle . . .*),

Paul's letter to the Ephesians (the letter begins with: *From Paul, who by God's will . . .*),

Paul's letter to the Philippians (the letter begins with: *From Paul and Timothy . . .*),

Paul's letter to the Colossians (the letter begins with: *From Paul, who by God's will . . .*)

Paul's First letter to the Thessalonians (the letter begins with: *From Paul, Silas, and Timothy – To . . .*)

Paul's Second letter to the Thessalonians (the letter begins with: *From Paul, Silas, and Timothy . . .*)

Paul's First letter to Timothy (the letter begin with: *From Paul, an apostle of Christ Jesus by . . .*)

Paul's Second Letter to Timothy (the letter begins with: *From Paul, an apostle of Christ Jesus . . .*)

Paul's letter to Titus (the letter begins with: *From Paul, a servant of God and an . . .*)

Paul's letter to Philemon (the letter begins with: *From Paul, a prisoner for the sake of . . .*)

Which is the hour for Prayer?

Three o'clock in the afternoon (*The Acts of the Apostles, Chapter 3, verse 1*)

Angels

As children, we were taught a prayer:

Angel of God

My guardian dear

To whom His love

Commits me here

Ever this day

Be at my side

To light and guard

To rule and guide. Amen.

Why were we taught this prayer? Are angels mentioned in the Holy Bible? This article is an attempt to answer the aforesaid questions.

Angels in the Four Gospels

Angel Gabriel announced the birth of John the Baptist to Zechariah *(Luke 1: 13)*. Angel Gabriel also announced the birth of Jesus to Mary *(Luke 1: 28 – 31)*.

Angel Gabriel occupies an important place.

Gabriel stands in the presence of God *(Luke 1: 19)*. According to *Tobit 12:15*, Raphael says, "I am Raphael, one of the seven angels who stand in the glorious presence of the Lord, ready to serve him".

Thus we can draw the inference that there are *seven angels who stand in the presence of the Lord* and Gabriel is one of them.

Angel Gabriel understands people and does not want to intimidate them.

When Zechariah saw angel Gabriel, he was alarmed and felt afraid. In fact, angel Gabriel said to Zechariah, *"Don't be afraid, Zechariah*! ..." *(Luke 1: 13)*. Gabriel's first words to Mary were: *"Peace be with you! The Lord is with you and has greatly blessed you!" (Luke 1 : 28).*

Angel Gabriel proves that God has sent him.

Because Zechariah initially found it difficult to believe Gabriel's words, Gabriel announced that Zechariah would be unable to speak and would remain silent until the day Gabriel's promise would come true. And it happened this way.

According to *Luke 2: 9 – 10*, when Jesus was born, an **angel of the Lord** appeared to some shepherds who were spending the night in the fields, taking care of their flocks and announced the birth of Lord Jesus Christ. The angel's first words to the shepherds were "*Don't be afraid!* I am here with good news for you, ...", and according to *Luke 2: 13*, a great **army of heaven's angels** appeared with the angel (who had announced the birth of Lord Jesus to the shepherds) singing praises to God.

According to *Matthew 1: 20*, when Joseph was contemplating on breaking his engagement to Mary privately, an **angel of the Lord** appeared to him in a dream and said, "Joseph, descendant of David, do not be afraid to take Mary to be your wife. For it is by the Holy Spirit that she has conceived. She will have a son, and you will name him Jesus – because he will save his people from their sins".

According to *Matthew 2: 13*, after the birth of Jesus, an **angel of the Lord** appeared to Joseph in a dream and advised Joseph to take baby Jesus and his mother and escape to Egypt (because Herod would be looking for the child in order to kill him). According to *Matthew 2: 19*, after the death of Herod, an **angel of the Lord** appeared to Joseph in a dream and advised Joseph to take baby Jesus and his mother back to the land of Israel.

Jesus was tempted by the Devil after spending forty days and nights without food. Jesus drove the Devil away and the **angels** came and helped Jesus *(Matthew 4: 1 – 11)*. The Devil had taken Jesus to Jerusalem the Holy City, set him on the highest point of the Temple, and asked Jesus to throw himself down quoting from the scripture, "God will give orders to his **angels** about you; they will hold you up with their hands, so that not even your feet will be hurt on the stones."

According to *Matthew 13: 41 – 42*, Jesus said, "the son of Man will send out his **angels** to gather up out of his Kingdom all those who cause people to sin and all others who do evil things, and they will throw them into the fiery furnace, where they will cry and grind their teeth". *Matthew 13: 49 – 50* also speak of the work of the **angels** at the end of the age.

Jesus said, "I assure you that whoever declares publicly that he belongs to me, the Son of Man will do the same for him before the **angels of God**. But whoever rejects me publicly, the Son of Man will also reject him before the **angels of God**" *(Luke 12: 8 – 9)*.

Before his arrest and crucifixion, when Jesus was praying at the Mount of Olives, asking his Father, "if you will, take this cup of suffering away from me. Not my will, however, but your will be done", an **angel from heaven** appeared to him and strengthened him *(Luke 22: 41 – 43).*

When Jesus was arrested, one of those who were with Jesus drew his sword and struck at the High Priest's slave, cutting off his ear. Jesus said, "Put your sword back in its place, all who take the sword will die by the sword. Don't you know that I could call on my Father for help, and at once he would send me more than twelve **armies of angels**?..." *(Matthew 26: 47 – 55).*

As Sunday morning was dawning after the crucifixion of Lord Jesus, Mary Magdalene and the other Mary went to look at the tomb. Suddenly there was a violent earthquake; an **angel of the Lord** came down from heaven, rolled the stone away, and sat on it. His appearance was like lightning, and his clothes were white as snow. The angel spoke to the women: "*You must not be afraid*, I know you are looking for Jesus, who was crucified. He is not here; he has been raised, just as he said. Come here and see the place where he was lying. Go quickly now, and tell his disciples, 'He has been raised from death, and now he is going to Galilee ahead of you; there you will see him!'" *(Matthew 28: 1 – 8).*

According to *John 20: 11 – 12,* Mary Magdalene bent over and looked into Jesus's tomb and saw **two angels** dressed in white, sitting where the body of Jesus had been laid, one at the head and the other at the feet.

It appears, that when people see an angel then they feel frightened, but the angel says, "You must not be afraid…".

Angels of God rejoice over a sinner who repents *(Luke 15: 10).* **Angels** do not marry and they do not die *(Luke 20: 36), (Mark 12: 24).* In the parable of the rich man and Lazarus, when

the poor man died, he was carried by the **angels** to sit beside Abraham at the feast in heaven *(Luke 16: 22)*. Angels take care of small children. Jesus said, "See that you don't despise any of these little ones. Their **angels in heaven**, I tell you, are always in the presence of my Father in heaven" *(Matthew 18:10 – 11)*. Thus we can draw the inference that in all seven angels look after all the children in this world. Angels serve Jesus. Jesus said to Nathanael and Philip, "I am telling you the truth: you will see heaven open and **God's angels** going up and coming down on the Son of Man" *(John 1: 51)*. Angels do the work of the Lord and they are very strong. According to *John 5: 4*, "For at intervals an **angel** descended into the pool and stirred the water. Whoever got in first after the agitation of the pool enjoyed healing, no matter what ailment he suffered". The bathing pool referred to herein is Bethzatha, which is near the Sheep Gate in Jerusalem and it has five porches.

[*Verse 8* in *The Letter from Jude* contains the name of chief angel **Michael**.]

Psalms: Interesting Facts

Verse 13 of Psalm 9: *"Be merciful to me, O Lord!"*

Verse 9 of Psalm 31: *"Be merciful to me, Lord, for I am in trouble; . . ."*

Psalm 51 begins with *"Be merciful to me, O God".*

Psalm 56 begins with *"Be merciful to me, O God".*

Psalm 57 begins with *"Be merciful to me, O God".*

Psalm 69 begins with *"Save me, O God!".*

Psalm 70 begins with *"Save me, O God!".*

Psalm 93 begins with *"The Lord is king".*

Psalm 99 begin with *"The Lord is king".*

Psalm 96 begins with *"Sing a new song to the Lord".*

Psalm 98 begins with *"Sing a new song to the Lord".*

Psalm 105 begins with *"Give thanks to the Lord".*

Psalm 107 begins with *"Give thanks to the Lord."*

Psalm 119 has 176 verses.

The last word of Psalm 125 is *'Israel'*.

The last word of Psalm 128 is *'Israel'*. The first word of Psalm 129 is *'Israel'*.

Psalm 29 begins with: Praise the LORD.

The last sentence of Psalm 41 is "Praise the LORD, the God of Israel! Praise him now and for ever!"

The term '*praise the LORD!*' appears in the first sentence of Psalm 95.

The first sentence of Psalm 103 is "Praise the LORD, my soul!"

The last sentence of Psalm 103 is "Praise the LORD, my soul!"

The first sentence of Psalm 104 is "Praise the LORD, my soul!"

The second last sentence of Psalm 104 is "Praise the LORD, my soul!"

The last sentence of Psalm 104 is "Praise the LORD!"

The last sentence of Psalm 105 is "Praise the LORD!"

The first sentence of Psalm 106 is "Praise the LORD!"

The last sentence of Psalm 106 is "Praise the LORD!"

The first sentence of Psalm 111 is "Praise the LORD!"

The first sentence of Psalm 112 is "Praise the LORD!"

The first sentence of Psalm 113 is "Praise the LORD!"

The last sentence of Psalm 113 is "Praise the LORD!"

The last sentence of Psalm 115 is "Praise the LORD!"

The first sentence of Psalm 117 is "Praise the LORD, all nations!"

The last sentence of Psalm 117 is "Praise the LORD!"

The term '*praise the Lord*' appears in the first sentence of Psalm 134.

The first sentence of Psalm 135 is: Praise the Lord!

The last sentence of Psalm 135 is: Praise the Lord!

Psalm 144 begins with: Praise the Lord

The first sentence of Psalm 146 is: Praise the Lord!

The last sentence of Psalm 146 is: Praise the Lord!

The first sentence of Psalm 147 is: Praise the Lord!

The last sentence of Psalm 147 is: Praise the Lord!

The first sentence of Psalm 148 is: Praise the Lord!

The last sentence of Psalm 148 is: Praise the Lord!

The first sentence of Psalm 149 is: Praise the Lord!

The last sentence of Psalm 149 is: Praise the Lord!

All the sentences of Psalm 150 begin with the word 'Praise'.

The first sentence of Psalm 150 is: Praise the Lord!

The last sentence of Psalm 150 is: Praise the Lord!

A Case Study of "Jesus Feeds Five Thousand Men"

Question. In how many Gospels is the miracle of Jesus feeding five thousand men recorded?

Answer. The miracle in which Jesus feeds five thousand men is recorded in

The Gospel according to Matthew (Chapter 14, verses 13 – 20)

The Gospel according to Mark (Chapter 6, verses 30 – 44)

The Gospel according to Luke (Chapter 9, verses 12 – 17), and

The Gospel according to John (Chapter 6, verses 1 – 13).

It is important to bear in mind that out of all the miracles which Jesus performed on earth only a few can be found in the four gospels (Matthew, Mark, Luke and John).

	Matthew	*Mark*	*Luke*	*John*
Background	When Jesus heard about the death of John the Baptist, he left in a boat and went to a lonely place by himself. The people heard about it, so they left their towns and followed him by land.	Jesus had sent his disciples two by two and had given them authority over the evil spirits. The apostles returned and told Jesus all they had done and taught. There were so many people coming and going that Jesus and his disciples didn't even have time to eat. So they started out in a boat by themselves for a lonely place. Many people saw Jesus and his disciples leaving. So they went from all the towns and ran ahead by land and reached the place ahead of Jesus and his disciples.	Jesus gave his twelve disciples power and authority to drive out all demons and to cure diseases. He sent them out to preach the Kingdom of God. The apostles came back and told Jesus everything they had done. Jesus took the apostles with him to a town called **Bethsaida**. When the crowds heard about it, they followed him.	Jesus had healed a man who had been ill for thirty-eight years. Jesus healed him on the Sabbath day. The Jewish authorities learnt of this and began to persecute Jesus. Jesus explained to the Jewish authorities, his own authority as the Son of God. After this, Jesus went across **Lake Galilee** (or, Lake Tiberias). Jesus **went up a hill** and sat down with his disciples. A large crowd followed Jesus.

	Matthew	*Mark*	*Luke*	*John*
Jesus's response	Jesus's heart was filled with pity for his followers, and he healed those who were ill.	Jesus's heart was filled with pity for the people, because they were like sheep without a shepherd.	Jesus welcomed the crowds, spoke to them about the Kingdom of God, and healed those who needed it.	The time for the Passover Festival was near. Jesus asked **Philip**, "Where can we buy enough food to feed all these people?"
Timing	That **evening** the disciples said to Jesus, "It is already very late, and this is a lonely place. Send the people away and let them go to the villages to buy food for themselves".	When it was **getting late**, his disciples said, "It is already very late, and this is a lonely place. Send the people away, and let them go to the nearby farms and villages in order to buy themselves something to eat".	When **the sun was beginning to set**, the twelve disciples came to Jesus and said, "Send the people away so that they can go the villages and farms round here and find food and lodging, because this is a lonely place".	
Money value of food		The disciples asked Jesus, "Do you want us to go and spend **two hundred silver coins on bread** in order to feed them?"		**Philip** said to Jesus, "For everyone to have even a little, it would take more than **two hundred silver coins to buy enough bread**".

	Matthew	*Mark*	*Luke*	*John*
Jesus's answer	"They don't have to leave. You yourselves give them something to eat!"	"You yourselves give them something to eat", Jesus answered.	Jesus said, "You yourselves give them something to eat".	

	Matthew	*Mark*	*Luke*	*John*
Food available	The disciples replied, "All we have here are five loaves and two fish".	When Jesus asked his disciples "How much bread have you got? Go and see". The disciples found out that they were having five loaves and also two fish.	The disciples answered, "All we have are five loaves and two fish. Do you want us to go and buy food for this whole crowd?"	**Andrew** said, "There is a boy here who has five loaves of barley bread and two fish. But they will certainly not be enough for all these people".

	Matthew	Mark	Luke	John
How Jesus fed the people?	Jesus ordered the people to sit down on the grass. He took the five loaves and the two fish, looked up to heaven, and gave thanks to God. He broke the bread and gave it to his disciples, and the disciples gave them to the people.	Jesus told his disciples to make all the people divide into groups and sit down on the green grass. So the people sat down in rows, in groups of a hundred and groups of fifty. Then Jesus took the five loaves and the two fish, looked up to heaven and gave thanks to God. He broke the loaves and gave them to his disciples to distribute to the people. He also divided the two fish among them all.	Jesus said to his disciples, "Make the people sit down in groups of about fifty each". Jesus took the five loaves and two fish, looked up to heaven, thanked God for them, broke them, and gave them to the disciples to distribute to the people.	Jesus said to his disciples, "Make the people sit down". Jesus took the bread, gave thanks to God, and distributed it to the people who were sitting there. He did the same with the fish.

	Matthew	*Mark*	*Luke*	*John*
Number of men who ate	The number of men who ate was about five thousand, not counting the women and children.	The number of men who were fed was five thousand.	About five thousand men.	About five thousand men.
Left over	The disciples took up twelve baskets full of what was left over.	The disciples took up twelve baskets full of what was left of the bread and the fish.	The disciples took up twelve baskets of what was left over.	When the people were all full, Jesus said to his disciples, "Gather the pieces left over; let us not waste any". So the disciples gathered the left over food and filled twelve baskets.
The next event	Jesus walks on the water.	Jesus walks on the water.	Peter's declaration about Jesus.	Jesus walks on the water.

Lessons learnt:

Jesus is grieved when he hears about the death of John the Baptist.

Jesus has pity on his followers and heals the people who are in need.

Jesus feeds his followers.

Jesus does not waste food.

Jesus thanks his Father before feeding his followers.

Jesus tests Philip.

Jesus takes care of those who follow him.

The disciples of Jesus were empowered to perform miracles: "You yourselves give them something to eat!"

The numbers which force us to ponder:

Five loaves of bread and Two fishes = (5 + 2) = 7. There are seven days in a week, seven continents in the world, seven colours in the rainbow.

Five thousand men: perhaps men eat **more** than women and children.

Twelve baskets of left-over food: Jesus had twelve disciples. Also reminds us of Twelve tribes of Israel. The number twelve appears several times in Leviticus (Chapter 24, verses 5 – 7).

A Case Study of "Jesus Feeds Four Thousand Men"

Question. *In how many Gospels is the miracle of Jesus feeding four thousand men recorded?*

Answer. The miracle in which Jesus feeds four thousand men is recorded in

The Gospel according to Matthew (Chapter 15, verses 32 – 38)

The Gospel according to Mark (Chapter 8, verses 1 – 10).

[N.B.: In contrast, the miracle in which Jesus feeds five thousand men, is recorded in the Gospels of Matthew, Mark, Luke and John.

It is important to bear in mind that out of all the miracles which Jesus performed on earth only a few can be found in the four gospels (Matthew, Mark, Luke and John).]

	Matthew	*Mark*
Background	Jesus left the territory near the cities of Tyre and Sidon and went along by Lake Galilee. Jesus climbed a hill and sat down. Large crowds came to Jesus, bringing with them the lame, the blind, the crippled, the dumb and many other sick people, whom they placed at Jesus' feet and Jesus healed them. Jesus called his disciples and said, "I feel sorry for these people, because they have been with me for **three days** and now have nothing to eat. I don't want to send them away without feeding them, for they might faint on their way home".	Jesus left the neighbourhood of Tyre and went on through Sidon to Lake Galilee, going by way of the territory of the Ten Towns. Some people brought to Jesus a man who was deaf and could hardly speak. Jesus took him off alone, away from the crowd. Jesus placed his fingers in the man's ears, spat, and touched the man's tongue. Then Jesus looked up to heaven, gave a deep groan, and said to the man, "*Ephphatha*", which means, "Open up!" Not long afterwards another large crowd came together. When the people had nothing left to eat, Jesus called the disciples to him and said, "I feel sorry for these people, because they have been with me for **three days** and now have nothing to eat. If I send them home without feeding them, they will faint as they go, because some of them have come a long way".

	Matthew	*Mark*
The question that the disciples asked	"Where will we find enough food in this desert to feed this crowd?"	"Where in this desert can anyone find enough food to feed all these people?"

	Matthew	*Mark*
The question that Jesus asked	"How much bread have you?"	"How much bread have you got?"
The answer that the disciples gave	"Seven loaves and a few small fish"	"Seven loaves"
How Jesus fed the people	Jesus ordered the crowd to sit down on the ground. Then he took the **seven loaves and the fish**, gave thanks to God, broke them, and gave them to the disciples; and the disciples gave them to the people.	Jesus ordered the crowd to sit down on the ground. Then he took the **seven loaves**, gave thanks to God, broke them, and gave them to his disciples to distribute to the crowd; and the disciples did so. They also had a few small fish. Jesus gave thanks for these and told the disciples to distribute them too.
Number of people who were fed	The number of men who ate was four thousand, not counting the women and children.	There were about four thousand people.
Left over	The disciples took up **seven** baskets full of pieces left over.	The disciples took up **seven** baskets full of pieces left over.

	Matthew	*Mark*
After feeding the crowd	Jesus sent the people away, got into a boat, and went to the territory of Magadan.	Jesus sent the people away and at once got into a boat with his disciples and went to the district of Dalmanutha.

Lessons learnt:

Jesus is concerned about his followers (they will faint as they go).

Jesus has pity on his followers and heals the people who are in need.

Jesus wants to feed his followers.

Jesus does not waste food.

Jesus thanks God before feeding his followers.

Jesus takes care of those who follow him.

Jesus had a very LOUD voice. More than four thousand people could hear Jesus when he (Lord Jesus) spoke. If a normal human being speaks (without the help of a microphone) in a room which houses barely a hundred people, I am not very sure if all the hundred people would be able to hear him at the same time and understand the message.

The numbers which force us to ponder:

Three days: Peter denied Lord Jesus thrice. Lord Jesus Christ rose from the dead on the third day. The number three can be found at several places in the four Gospels.

Seven loaves of bread. There are seven days in a week, seven continents in the world, seven colours in the rainbow.

Four thousand men: perhaps men eat **more** than women and children. If each man was married, and each man had brought his wife along then there could have been four thousand women. If each couple was having two children, then there might have been eight thousand children. In some cases, other female members such as sister(s), mother, aunt(s) might have accompanied the men.

Seven baskets of left-over food: The number seven appears several times in the Bible. Jesus does not want to waste food.

Question. Is it possible to feed four thousand men with seven loaves and few fishes?

Answer. When the disciples asked Jesus, "Who, then, can be saved?", Jesus said, "This is impossible for man, but for God everything is possible" (*Matthew 19: 25 – 26)*. A reading of the Holy Bible will convince us that Jesus can do what is impossible for man.

Question. Could God have created the world in six days?

Answer. According to 2 Peter 3: 8, "But do not forget one thing, my dear friends! There is no difference in the Lord's sight between one day and a thousand years; to him the two are the same".

It is important to understand that Peter does not say that 1 day = 1000 years or 1000 years = 1 day. Peter says that there is no difference in the Lord's sight between one day and a thousand years. An interpretation could be that God can see a thousand years at a time just like God may see a single day { in order to understand the phrase, an analogy can be used: just like we can watch a second pass by or a day pass by, God can watch 1000 years, but we cannot watch even a century (if there are exceptions, then I am not aware of those exceptions). }

According to Psalm 90: 4, "A thousand years to you are like one day; they are like yesterday, already gone, like a short hour in the night".

This could mean that God knows whatever has happened in the preceding 1000 years.

It is possible that Peter might have read the Psalm and echoed a sentence from the Psalm.

A Few Interesting Religious Books

Didachē: contains 16 enriching chapters pertaining to morals, ethics and church practice.

The Epistle of Barnabas

The Shepherd of Hermas

[Note: There are many books in this world. I (the author of this book) am not forcing / or trying to force anyone to read or not read any book.]

www.ingramcontent.com/pod-product-compliance
Lightning Source LLC
LaVergne TN
LVHW041235150826
845673LV00008B/2388

* 9 7 9 8 8 9 6 7 3 8 4 1 1 *